Create a Bug Out Bag for Emergency Survival Situations

Professional Ethics: 100 Tips to Improve Your Professional Life

Richard G Lowe, Jr

Create a Bug Out Bag for Emergency Survival Situations

How Preppers Prepare Their Go Bags for Evacuations to Survive Disasters

Volume 2 of the Disaster Preparation and Survival series

Published by The Writing King
www.thewritingking.com

Create a Bug Out Bag for Emergency Survival Situations

Copyright © 2016 by Richard G Lowe, Jr.

All rights reserved. No part of this publication may be reproduced, stored in a retrieval system, or transmitted by any means – electronic, mechanical, photographic (photocopying), recording, or otherwise – without prior permission in writing from the author.

Although every precaution has been taken to verify the accuracy of the information contained herein, the author and publisher assume no responsibility for any errors or omissions. No liability is assumed for damages that may result from the use of information contained within.

Trademarked names appear throughout this book. Rather than use a trademark symbol with every occurrence of a trademarked name, names are used in an editorial fashion, with no intention of infringement of the respective owner's trademark.

Cover Artist: theamateurzone

ASIN: B012IV39DS
ISBN: 978-1-943517-79-4 (Hardcover)
ISBN: 978-1-943517-78-7 (Paperback)
ISBN: 978-1-943517-08-4 (eBook)

Table of Contents

Table of Contents i
Introduction v
Your bug out bag 1
Food and water 3
    Water purification tablets 3
    Meals Ready to eat 4
    Food bars 5
Light, power, and warmth 7
    Flashlights 7
    Batteries 8
    Waterproof matches 9
    Clothing 10
Protection from the environment 11
    Masks 11
    Goggles 12
    Sunscreen 13
    Hats 13
    Ponchos 14
    Sleeping blankets 14
Toiletries 17
    Toothpaste 17
    Toothbrush 17
    Floss 17
    Mouthwash 17

Table of Contents

    Shampoo and conditioner 18

    Lip balm 18

    Toilet paper 18

    Feminine supplies 18

    Trash bags 19

Medical 21

    Alcohol wipes 22

    Bandages 22

    Tape 23

    Gauze 23

    Vitamin C 23

    Multivitamins 23

    Hand antiseptic 23

    Scissors and tweezers 24

    Special medical supplies 24

Miscellaneous Equipment 25

    Can Opener 25

    Keys 25

    Whistle 25

    Knife 25

    Radio 26

Documentation 27

    City or county information 28

    Paper and pens 29

    Small camera 29

Table of Contents

Conclusion..31
About the Author 33
Books by Richard G Lowe Jr. 37
Additional Resources 43
Premium Writing Services 45

Introduction

Disaster can strike at any time. Sometimes, as with a hurricane, you may get some notice; other times, in the case of a fire or an earthquake, you'll receive no warning at all.

Most of the time, the disaster will leave your home and the surrounding area more or less intact. I've been in several earthquakes that damaged the furniture and windows of my apartment, but otherwise, everything was fine. When I lived in the mountains, there were forest fires that burned close to where I lived, but fortunately, there was no damage to my residence.

Regardless of whether your residence is damaged or not, you may be required to evacuate the area. This can happen for many reasons.

When I lived in the mountains, several evacuations were implemented because it appeared to the authorities that there was some danger that a fire would burn through the town. Fortunately, the fire department was able control fire before that happened.

After a disaster like a chemical spill, the authorities may order residents to evacuate immediately. It may be several weeks or longer before anyone is allowed back into their homes.

Even local police action due to criminal activity can require a quick evacuation. Police generally ask residents to stay in their homes during these situations.

Introduction

In the United States, plenty of warning is given before a hurricane occurs. In these cases, authorities may order mass evacuations of whole cities.

When you are ordered to evacuate—or if you evacuate on your own free will—you generally don't have a lot of time to gather your belongings and the things you'll need. You may have just a few minutes to get out of your home.

The best preparation for evacuation is to create what is called a bug out bag. These are also known as go-bags, as in, "grab it and go!"

If you haven't already created your bug out bag, you need to as soon as possible. Use this book as a guide to stocking and maintaining your bug out bag over time.

I hope you enjoy what I've written and find it to be of some value. If you would like to send me a note about this book, feel free to write me at rich@thewritingking.com. If you enjoyed the book, please write a positive review.

Your bug out bag

The first thing you'll need to purchase is a bag of some kind. The bag should be able to hold all of the necessary emergency supplies in a readily accessible fashion.

I recommend using a moderately large duffle bag, preferably equipped with wheels and a handle. These are typically used for traveling and can be found at any store that sells luggage or camping supplies. If you prefer, you can use a high quality backpack or a standard duffle bag without wheels, but a bug out bag can be heavy. You may have to carry it long distances. By purchasing one with wheels and a handle, you can drag it behind you just like people drag luggage behind them when they're at the airport.

Purchase a bug out bag that is made of durable material so that it can take some punishment.

These bags are typically not waterproof. Thus, items that can be damaged by water should be stored in sealable plastic bags or boxes. This way, if your bag gets wet the contents will not be destroyed.

Store liquids or powders in sealable plastic bags as well. That way, leaks will not ruin everything else in your bug out bag.

My duffle bag on wheels also has some external pockets with zippers. These pockets make smaller items readily accessible and remove the hassle of removing all of the bag's contents to find them. The external pockets are perfect for flashlights, food bars, and rain ponchos.

Your bug out bag

The bag itself is probably going to be the most expensive part of your project. Don't skimp on this; during a disaster, you don't want your bag to fall apart. That's when you need it most.

Food and water

It's wise to include enough food to last a day or two. A few MREs (Meals Ready to Eat), granola, and food bars can help when you need to evacuate. It may be difficult to find food at stores during the chaos of the evacuation. Having a little bit of food in your bag can help you overcome this problem.

I don't recommend including much water, as it can leak and damage the contents of your bag. Water is heavy; you can't carry very much of it. For the water you do include, remember to rotate it according to the dates on the bottles, as it can become contaminated and undrinkable.

In my bag, I include four water bottles, just enough to provide for a day at the most.

While carrying an abundance of water in your bag has its downsides, it is always a good idea to bring some water with you. Keep several 1gallon jugs near your bug out bag and throw those jugs into the trunk of your car when you evacuate. A case of individual water bottles or one of those 5 gallon jugs that can be delivered to your doorstep are suitable alternatives to the 1 gallon jugs.

WATER PURIFICATION TABLETS

Water can become contaminated with bacterial or viral pathogens. Water purification tablets are an excellent way to kill pathogens and make water drinkable.

You can purchase a bottle of 50 tablets from any store that sells camping goods. Read the label thoroughly, as

Food and water

instructions can vary from brand to brand. Make sure to also read the cautions, as the chemicals in these tablets can affect people differently.

I keep two bottles of these tablets in my bug out bag, which should purify 100 liters of water. That works out to about 26 gallons.

Generally, one tablet will purify about a liter of water. You must understand, though, that these tablets only work on biological contamination. They will not help if the water contains dangerous chemicals or other substances.

Wait about an hour after putting the tablet into the water before drinking.

You can use these tablets for water that has been contaminated by flooding from heavy rains or overflowing rivers. Also use them if your pipes have been damaged by earthquakes or fires, or if water been standing for long periods of time.

If water contains sediment, first filter it through a fine cloth. Once you filter out the sediment, you can use a purification tablet or two to ensure any bacteria are killed.

MEALS READY TO EAT

One of the best ways to keep a supply of food available in your bug out bag is to purchase a case of MREs (Meals Ready to Eat). These are self-contained meals that can be eaten straight out of the bag or box. These meals are designed to last years without refrigeration, and if you store them in a cool place, they will last over a decade.

Food and water

Each MRE comes in a tough package designed for travel and outdoor conditions. Inside the package, there is one entrée and a side dish such as rice, corn, or fruit. They also come with pepper and salt, some candy, and even sauce packets. If you prefer hot food, you can purchase them with chemical heaters for a small extra charge.

The military designed MREs to provide one-third of a person's daily caloric intake (1,250 for each pack), vitamins, and minerals. A person should be able to survive on three MREs per day, plus water.

Many companies sell MREs by the case or in multiple-case lots. I purchased six cases of 12 meals from MRESTAR at http://www.mre-meals.net/. I highly recommend the products from this company.

If you want to learn more about MREs, a good place to start is http://www.mreinfo.com/. That site contains full descriptions of all of the different options available.

You can store the case in a readily accessible area, preferably near your bug out bag, and throw it into your car when you evacuation. I keep six MREs in my bug out bag. They are relatively light—although they do take up quite a bit of space—and packing them in my bag ensures I have at least two days' worth of food if I have to evacuate on a moment's notice and cannot pack my case of MREs.

FOOD BARS

It's a good idea to store a couple dozen food bars in your bug out bag. There are some different options available, from

Food and water

simple granola bars to expensive food bars designed to remain edible virtually forever.

In my bag, I keep 12 regular granola bars and 12 granola bars mixed with various kinds of nuts. Since I also have quite a few MREs in my bag, I include the food bars because they are higher in carbohydrates.

Remember that food bars need to be rotated. Printed on each bar is an expiration date. Generally, these dates are about six months from the date of purchase.

As you buy new bars, take the old ones out of your bag and replace them with the new ones. Then you can go ahead and use the old ones as part of your normal eating routine. If you don't do this, you may find yourself with stale or even inedible bars when you need them the most.

Light, power, and warmth

Electric power gets to your home via a complex system of towers, cables, tunnels, substations, and generators. Each of these components is vulnerable to the effects of the disaster.

An earthquake can knock down towers, cause trees to fall across cables, and destroy substations and generators. The electric grid can adapt to a certain number of failures, but a major disaster is likely to overwhelm the system and cause the power to fail.

As you plan your bug out bag, take into account that you may be without electricity for a few days to a few weeks.

FLASHLIGHTS

Flashlights are important. Without electricity, you will find it difficult to maneuver around your home in the dark.

If you'd like to do a quick experiment, wait until dark, then turn off all the breakers in your breaker box (excluding the ones leading to your appliances like your refrigerator). Take a look around your home. You'll quickly understand why you need to keep a few flashlights in your bag.

In these modern times, we've become accustomed to having lights everywhere. I know most of the appliances in my home have tiny little lights to show that they're working. I have a couple of lights plugged into the wall; they switch on in the evening and act as night lights. Clocks, computers, and other electronics have dimly lit panels.

Light, power, and warmth

Without power, all of these lights are gone. It's amazing how dark everything is without all electronics turned on.

If you walk outside in the dark, you may need a flashlight to be able to see where you're going.

Many people use candles instead of flashlights in the event of a power outage. I caution against that. Open flames are not wise after disasters have occurred. The gas can be leaking, an animal can knock over a candle, or something can fall on the open flame start a fire.

I keep two regular size flashlights inside of my bug out bag. Both of them are water resistant, so they will operate even in the rain or in wet conditions. Since I may have to use the flashlights quickly, I store them in the bag with batteries inside. That way I don't have to fumble around in the dark, trying to figure out how to put batteries into the flashlight.

I also stock my bag with four smaller penlights. Each of these requires two AA batteries. They are not as powerful as the larger flashlights, but their batteries tend to last longer, and they are much lighter. This makes it easier to carry them in a disaster.

BATTERIES

Stock at least enough batteries in your bug out bag to replace the ones in your flashlights at least twice. For example, I have two flashlights in my bag, each of which requires two D cell batteries. Thus, I stock eight spare D-cell batteries in my bag.

Remember that batteries expire and need to be rotated on occasion. In my home, I don't have any other needs for D-cell

Light, power, and warmth

batteries at all. So in my case rather than being a case of rotating the batters, I must ensure they are not expired.

In other words, replace the batteries well before they get to the expiration date.

Batteries are relatively heavy, so you don't want to store too many of them in your bag. If you do, you may find that it's too heavy to carry.

WATERPROOF MATCHES

There may be times during a disaster when you need to start a fire. This could be as simple as lighting a cigarette, lighting a candle, or starting a fire in the backyard so you can cook.

In a disaster, it's quite possible that the electricity and gas will no longer work. This means you will be unable to cook with your stove, the light bulbs will no longer shine, and you may not even have hot water.

In addition, it could be so dangerous that you need to turn off the gas or electricity. This could happen if you believe there is a gas leak, or if there has been damage to the electrical wiring by a flood or an earthquake.

The inside of your home or car may be drenched due to excessive rain, leaky pipes, or floodwaters. If you have any matches, you may find that they are soaked and can no longer be used to start a fire.

You can find boxes of waterproof matches at your local camping supply shop or any store that sells camping supplies.

Light, power, and warmth

These are wooden matches with the flammable tip soaked with waterproof material.

These waterproof matches come in small boxes, and they are very light. I keep a dozen boxes in my bug out bag.

CLOTHING

Imagine that a disaster has occurred. The authorities have ordered an evacuation, and you have to leave your home quickly. It's raining outside. In the time it takes you to get from your home to the car, you're soaked.

Since you are in a hurry, the only thing you were able to grab was your bug out bag. Wouldn't it be nice to have a change of clothes in that bag?

In my bag, I keep a pair of jeans, a shirt, a few pair of underclothes, and a couple of changes of socks. This way, if I have to leave in a hurry, I know I have clothes to change into once I get to where I am going.

While it is wise to keep a change of clothing in your bug out bag, remember that you don't want it to be too heavy. The most essential piece of clothing to put in your bag is a couple of changes of socks, followed by your underclothes, and then a good pair of jeans.

The clothes don't have to be sexy or stylish. In my bag, I keep a pair of older jeans and an old work shirt that would work in just about any circumstance.

Protection from the environment

In the event of an evacuation, you're going to find yourself needing protection from the environment. In some cases, all you need is protection from the sun with a hat, sunscreen, and lip balm.

However, disasters tend to throw lots of dust and debris into the air. Because of this, you may want to pack a respiratory mask in your bag. You can include goggles to protect your eyes, a poncho to keep the rain off your clothes, and a space-age blanket to stay warm.

MASKS

After any disaster, the air may be full of contaminants. For example, there could be concrete dust from a collapsed building or loose asbestos from a wall that was destroyed in an earthquake.

At the low-end, home improvement stores carry inexpensive dust masks. You can also find these in the first aid section of some stores. These are disposable, uncomfortable, absorb sweat, and become unusable quickly. They also don't protect you from small particles. They have the advantage that they are very lightweight and inexpensive.

Slightly more expensive, but of a much better quality, are dust masks called particulate respirators. A rating of N95 is recommended. These will fit better on your face—although a beard or mustache makes them less effective—and it will give you better protection from dust and debris. You can find these online in packs of 20 for less than $20.

Protection from the environment

If you are worried about particulate matter and dust, perhaps because of allergies or a medical condition, then you might prefer a heavy-duty respirator. Painters and construction workers wear these types of masks. They are very expensive, in the $20-$40 range, but they last virtually forever. They do a pretty good job of filtering out just about everything, including dust, chemicals, bacteria, and viruses.

Another option is a product called ReadiMask. These are lightweight, protect the eyes as well as the lungs, and have a medical adhesive seal. You can find these on the Internet for about $10 each. There are two sizes: one for adults and one for children.

If you choose the inexpensive, disposable masks, include a box of them in your bug out bag. If, on the other hand, you purchase a respirator or a ReadiMask, you'll need one for each person.

GOGGLES

Including a pair of goggles in your bug out bag can be useful in situations where you need to protect your eyes. For example, a storm or hurricane may launch large amounts of debris in the air. Wearing a pair of goggles can save your eyes from damage.

Goggles can be found online or at any home improvement store. If you wear glasses, try them on before making a purchase to make sure your glasses fit underneath the goggles.

Protection from the environment

SUNSCREEN

The bright sun can be a problem if you're caught outdoors after an emergency or disaster. If, for example, the evacuation center consists of a large parking lot, you may find yourself exposed to the open sun. The same issue can result if you have to walk for long distances.

Sunlight can cause numerous short-term problems. If your body is warm, you will produce more sweat, which means you lose water. This can happen even if it's very cold; in that case, sweating is even more dangerous because it causes you to lose heat and can lead to hypothermia.

Keep a bottle of high SPF sunscreen in your bug out bag. I would recommend at least 50 SPF. If you have to be outside for any length of time, put the sunscreen on all exposed areas of your skin.

Because sunscreen is a liquid, be sure you store the bottle inside of a plastic bag that seals. That way, if the sunscreen leaks you won't have it all over the inside of your bag.

HATS

The hot sun shining down upon your head can cause your body to lose a lot of heat and moisture due to excessive sweating. In addition, the sun can cause sunburns on your scalp that can be very uncomfortable.

Keep an extra hat in your bug out bag. Make sure it's made of a nice, thick material with a brim, or that is long enough to cover the top of your ears. Fishing or hunting hats are perfect, as these are already made for this purpose.

Protection from the environment

PONCHOS

During an emergency, is possible that you could need to travel or move about when it's raining. The problem with getting wet is that the water tends to soak through your clothes, causing your body to lose heat quickly. It's important to remain as dry as possible during an emergency, or to dry off and remove wet clothing as soon as you can.

Most bug out bags are not large enough to fit clothing like coats and jackets. During an evacuation, I would make it a point to grab my coat in addition to the bug out bag as I left the building. Of course, this can be forgotten or overlooked in the chaos of an emergency, or your jacket or coat may not be where you expect them to be.

You can purchase ponchos online or from a store that sells camping supplies. These are made of thin plastic and are very light weight.

You should include a couple of these ponchos in your bug out bag. They don't take up much space, and they don't weigh very much. If you have to evacuate and are caught in the rain, they can be very helpful in keeping your clothing and your body dry.

SLEEPING BLANKETS

Obviously, you can't put a standard size sleeping blanket in your bug out bag. There wouldn't be enough space. However, you can include several space age blankets.

You can buy these online or in just about any store that sells camping supplies. They are very small and light. You should include several of them in your bug out bag.

Protection from the environment

These bags consist of a very thin plastic film covered with a coating of vaporized aluminum. These bags reflect heat, which assists the body in staying warm.

As you move about, water evaporates from your skin in the form of sweat. Sweating uses a lot of energy and lowers the body temperature. These space age blankets increase the humidity of the air next to your skin, which helps keep your body warm.

When your body contacts another surface, the heat from your body transfers between you and the other surface. If you sit on a cold bench, the heat from your backside is transferred to the bench, and you become colder. This phenomenon is made worse if you are in a cold wind. The wind will take the warmth from your body; this is referred to as the wind-chill factor. Space age blankets reduce this phenomenon.

Finally, heat radiates from your body into the surrounding space. By covering yourself with one of these blankets, much of the heat is reflected back to your body.

Space age blankets lessen the effects of all three of these phenomenon and keep you warmer.

Toiletries

If you are forced to evacuate quickly, you probably aren't going to have time to grab toiletries on your way out. Thus, it's probably a good idea to include a few things in your bug out bag to help with your personal comfort and cleanliness. Including things like a toothbrush and dental floss can help soothe the mind, as the presence of a daily routine such as oral care brings some normality to the situation.

Since some of these things are liquid or cream, put them into a 1 quart, sealable plastic bag. If anything leaks, your bug out bag will not be covered with toothpaste or some other liquid.

TOOTHPASTE
You can include small sized travel toothpaste or grab one of the smaller sizes of your favorite one. I find the travel sizes to be extraordinarily expensive and tend to gravitate to the smaller sizes of toothpaste.

TOOTHBRUSH
Pick up a multipack of toothbrushes and include it in your bug out bag.

FLOSS
Dental floss is inexpensive, light, and small. It should be included in your bug out bag.

MOUTHWASH
A small travel sized bottle of mouthwash is useful. While I usually find travel sized items unnecessarily expensive, I tend

Toiletries

to use the travel size mouthwash. Regular size bottles are too large and heavy.

SHAMPOO AND CONDITIONER

You can buy a travel size bottle of shampoo and conditioner, or acquire them for free the next time you stay in a hotel. Generally, a hotel will be happy to give you a couple of extra ones if you ask nicely.

While it might seem extravagant to include shampoo and conditioner in your bug out bag, two small bottles won't occupy much space and are not very heavy. I've found that washing up after a couple of days stuffed in a car or jammed into a refugee center is good for morale.

LIP BALM

Be sure to include a few tubes of lip balm. They're inexpensive and very light. This can help protect your lips from the harsh environment.

TOILET PAPER

If you have room in your bug out bag, include a few rolls of toilet paper. While two rolls may take up a bit of space, the evacuation center may run out, or you may find yourself stranded in your car for some period of time. Without this, you may find things getting a bit messy and unclean.

FEMININE SUPPLIES

If you're a woman or have women in your family, be sure to include feminine supplies in your bug out bag.

Toiletries

TRASH BAGS

Be sure to pack a dozen trash bags in your bag. Trash bags are useful for a variety of things during an evacuation. You may find yourself foraging for or scavenging items to help you survive, or you may just want a place to store your trash so the area doesn't stink.

Also, you can use trash bags to store things that shouldn't get wet. For example, any clothes that you manage to grab during an evacuation will remain dry inside a trash bag.

Medical

It is very likely that medical problems will occur in any emergency or disaster situation. During an earthquake, items and debris are thrown all over the place; buildings collapse, glass flies through the air, and books fall off of shelves. Hurricanes can smash windows, and belongings fly around as if they were possessed.

Minor cuts, bruises, and abrasions will almost inevitably occur in an emergency disaster scenario. Significant wounds and damage to the body are also likely.

Thus, it is wise to include a few medical supplies in your bug out bag. Some people prefer to purchase one of the premade first aid kits available at the supermarket. I don't like these kits. They tend to have cheap materials, too much of stuff that's never used, and not enough of the items that are needed.

For example, some of them include a pair of tweezers or scissors, and these are, to say the least, a bit of a joke. They also contain, as a rule, several different kinds of analgesics such as aspirin, acetaminophen, or ibuprofen. Most people tend to have a preference as to which kind of analgesic to use and don't need all three.

These premade kids also don't have enough bandages of the size is normally needed, and the antibiotic creams are in inadequate, single use containers.

I've individually purchased the specific items that I feel are necessary for an emergency, and I store them in a smaller

Medical

bag inside of my bug out bag. This way, I know that I have exactly what I need and not the low quality, ridiculously small quantities that are included in the premade kits.

Whether it's premade or homemade, ensure you have first aid supplies in your bug out bag. You would be wise to leave a first aid kit in your car, at the office, and anywhere else that you spend long periods of time.

ALCOHOL WIPES

Anything from minor cuts and bruises to major wounds can happen during a disaster. To help with the possibility of infection, you can purchase a box of a 150 individually packaged alcohol wipes for just a few dollars. You can find these at any store that sells first-aid supplies.

Include one of these boxes in your bug out bag. That way, you can sterilize any minor scrapes and cuts.

BANDAGES

I don't worry about all the fancy sizes of bandages that line the shelves at drug stores. In my bug out bag, I include two boxes of bandages: a standard size and extra-large size. I also include a box of butterfly bandages. These are useful for cuts on the hands.

I have found the other sizes tend to go to waste. Just two sizes will handle virtually every scenario. The standard size bandage is good for normal cuts and scrapes, while the larger size is useful for more significant wounds.

Be careful not to buy the super cheap boxes of bandages. Spend a little extra money and get the higher quality. I have found that the cheap, generic brands tend to not last as long when in storage.

Tape

Include a roll of medical adhesive tape, which you can purchase from any store that sells first-aid supplies. It's a good idea to use paper tape if you can to avoid possible allergic reactions.

Gauze

You can purchase a box of individually wrapped gauze squares in packs of 20 to 50. These are used for covering larger wounds, and you use the tape to hold gauze down to the skin. In my bag, I have a box of twenty 2" x 2" squares.

Also include a roll of gauze. These are 2 inches to 4 inches wide. Get whatever size you feel comfortable with.

Vitamin C

My bug out bag medical kit includes a bottle of vitamin C tablets. Disasters put extra stress on the body. Vitamin C can be helpful to ward off infections and strengthen the immune system.

Multivitamins

Since it may not be possible to eat properly during an evacuation or disaster, my bug out bag also includes a bottle of multivitamins.

Hand antiseptic

I also keep a bottle of hand antiseptic in my bug out bag. Because the utilities—including water and sewage—may not be working after a disaster, the possibility of infection is much

Medical

higher. I have a large bottle that is stored in a sealable plastic bag to protect from possible leakage.

SCISSORS AND TWEEZERS

Purchase a quality set of scissors (not the junk ones that are included with your premade first-aid kit) and store them safely in your bug out bag. Keep it closed with a rubber band and wrap a piece of electrical tape around the point.

It's a good idea to include a pair of tweezers, which can be useful for pulling out splinters in an emergency.

SPECIAL MEDICAL SUPPLIES

If you have a special medical condition, be sure to include the supplies you need in your bug out bag. In the case of diabetes, for example, purchase an extra glucose meter and a bottle of strips and store them in your bag. Glucose meters are inexpensive; you can usually pick them up for between $20 and $30. The strips, on the other hand, can be very expensive.

If you have any medications that you need, try and keep a few days' worth in your bug out bag. Rotate them with your normal supply on a regular basis so they don't expire.

Miscellaneous Equipment

There are a few other things that you should include in your bug out bag. A can opener and a knife are essential, and no bug out bag should be without them. A copy of your keys can be useful, and a whistle can help you get out of a tight situation. Another useful item to consider is a hand cranked radio.

CAN OPENER

Purchase a good quality can opener that also includes a bottle opener. This will allow you to open any canned goods you have stocked in your bug out bag, or that you find along the way.

KEYS

Another useful thing to include in your bug out bag is a copy of your keys. You should include your house key, car key, and the other keys that you use on a regular basis. This this ensures you have these keys available even if you lose your keychain during evacuation.

WHISTLE

A whistle is useful. If you need to get someone's attention, you can use the whistle. If you were stuck inside a collapsed house, or if you saw a police officer at a distance, you could use the whistle to get someone's attention.

KNIFE

It's wise to include a small folding knife (a pocketknife) in your bug out bag. You can purchase them at any store that sells

Miscellaneous Equipment

camping goods. Get whatever size knife you feel comfortable with.

RADIO

You can get a hand cranked or battery powered radio online or from any survival goods store. Sometimes stores that stock camping goods will also sell this type of radio.

These are pretty simple to use. They have a crank, which you rapidly turn for several minutes. Turning the crank charges a battery, and then you can listen to the radio.

Radios of this type include, at the very least, an AM band, FM band, and the weather channel.

By including a radio in your bug out bag, you ensure that you can receive official announcements if needed. Generally, the authorities make these announcements, and they include closings, delays, evacuation orders, and severe weather warnings.

Documentation

Gather your important documents and makes copies of them. Put them all in a waterproof bag or container, then store that in your bug out bag.

The documents you need to include are:

- Your passport and visa
- Driver's licenses
- Birth, death, and marriage certificates
- Bank account numbers, preferably on a copy of a canceled check for each account
- Statements for each of your bank accounts, credits cards, money market accounts, etc.
- Copies of your automobile, medical, life, and home insurance policies
- Any military or other IDs you might have
- A recent photo of each family member
- Health, dental, and prescription cards for each family member
- A list of medicines and allergies for each person
- Paystub
- If you own a gun, include a copy of your license to carry if required

There is no telling what you will need in a disaster, so go through your important documents and decide if anything else would be useful.

Be aware of the security of these documents. Keep your go-bag secure, just as you would your wallet or purse. These

Documentation

papers are sensitive, personal information and it's important that it not fall into the wrong hands.

However, during a severe emergency, the most beneficial place for these documents to be is within your bug out bag.

CITY OR COUNTY INFORMATION

Many cities and counties have websites that go into great detail about plans for disasters. They often include evacuation instructions, emergency procedures, and lists of pre-assigned evacuation centers.

Make it a point to occasionally take a look at these websites. First of all, this will help you understand what you need to do in a disaster situation. Second, these sites often have newsletters that you can receive in the mail or via email. Subscribe to any of these and keep printed copies of a couple of the most recent editions in your bug out bag.

These websites frequently have a place for you to enter your contact information. They will send you via email occasional newsletters and information that's useful for disaster warnings so you can have time to prepare.

Often, you can enter your phone number and receive text messages of anything you need to know during a disaster.

If your city or county offers these kinds of services, take advantage of them. They will send out advance warnings of events like hurricanes and tornadoes. The newsletters and information on the website are invaluable.

Documentation

PAPER AND PENS

You should include a spiral-bound notebook with a hard cover inside your bug out bag. This will be useful if you have to take directions, record addresses, and take notes of orders given by the authorities.

Make sure your notebook is stored in a waterproof plastic bag that can be sealed to protect it from any possible water damage.

Throw a handful of pens in your bag as well so you have something to write with when you need it.

SMALL CAMERA

I recommend that you include a small camera in your bug out bag. You can use this to document anything that you need to record during the emergency. This can be useful if you need to submit an insurance claim, as it to help prove damages.

As you inspect the damage caused by the disaster, taking photographs is a good way to document what you find. This can help you organize your inspection, and it can be useful in the future.

Photographing is also a good way to calm the nerves, at least in my experience. I find it is a way to detach from the chaos that has just occurred. Other people may have different opinions, but that's what a camera does for me.

Most cameras today come with a video option, which is useful to record encounters with other people and confrontations with officials and police. For example, if the police order your car shoved off the road, you can document that order on video

Documentation

for use later, perhaps in a court of law or for your insurance company.

If it's possible, make sure that you get a camera that accepts normal, non-rechargeable batteries. Keep a few of these batteries in your bug out bag. Since the power may be out, you may not be able to recharge batteries during the disaster.

Photographing is also a good way to calm the nerves, at least in my experience. I find it is a way to extrovert from the chaos it just occurred. Other people may have different opinions, but that's what a camera does for me.

Most cameras today come with a video option, which is useful to record things such as encounters with other people and confrontations with officials and police. For example, if the police order your car shoved off the road you can document that order on video for use later, perhaps in a court of law or for your insurance company.

If it's possible, make sure that you get a camera that accepts normal, non-rechargeable batteries. Keep a few of these batteries in your bug out bag. Since the power may be out, you may not be able to recharge batteries during the disaster.

Conclusion

You can be prepared for emergencies. One of the best ways to prepare for any disaster is to create a bug out bag. This is a large bag, preferably with wheels and a handle, which contains the emergency supplies you will need to survive for a day or two away from home.

If you are ordered to evacuate, or if you decide conditions are too dangerous to remain, the first thing to do is grab your bug out bag and throw it into the car. If you have time, also grab a few gallons of water and any canned goods that you can snatch up.

If you have to leave in a hurry, having a complete bug out bag in an accessible location can save your life, or at least make it easier for you to survive.

Before you go

If you scroll to the last page in this eBook, you will have the opportunity to leave feedback and share the book with Before You Go. I'd be grateful if you turned to the last page and shared the book.

Also, if you have time, please leave a review. Positive reviews are incredibly useful. If you didn't like the book, please email me at rich@thewritingking.com and I'd be happy to get your input.

About the Author

https://www.linkedin.com/in/richardlowejr
Feel free to send a connection request

Follow me on Twitter: @richardlowejr

Richard Lowe has leveraged more than 35 years of experience as a Senior Computer Manager and Designer at four companies into that of a bestselling author, blogger, ghostwriter, and public speaker. He has written hundreds of articles for blogs and ghostwritten more than a dozen books and has published manuscripts about computers, the Internet, surviving disasters, management, and human rights. He is currently working on a ten-volume science fiction series – the Peacekeeper Series – to be published at the rate of three volumes per year, beginning in 2016.

Richard started in the field of Information Technology, first as the Vice President of Consulting at Software Techniques, Inc. Because he craved action, after six years he moved on to work for two companies at the same time: he was the Vice President of Consulting at Beck Computer Systems and the Senior Designer at BIF Accutel. In January 1994, Richard found a home at Trader Joe's as the Director of Technical Services and Computer Operations. He remained with that incredible company for almost 20 years before taking an early retirement to begin a new life as a professional writer. He is currently the CEO of The Writing King, a company that provides all forms of writing services, the owner of The EBay King, and a Senior Branding Expert for LinkedIn Makeover. You can find a current list of all books on his Author Page and

About the Author

take a look at his exclusive line of coloring books at The Coloring King.

Richard has a quirky sense of humor and has found that life is full of joy and wonder. As he puts it, "This little ball of rock, mud, and water we call Earth is an incredible place, with many secrets to discover. Beings fill our corner of the universe, and some are happy, and others are sad, but each has their unique story to tell."

His philosophy is to take life with a light heart, and he approaches each day as a new source of happiness. Evil is ignored, discarded, or defeated; good is helped, enriched, and fulfilled. One of his primary interests is to educate people

About the Author

about their human rights and assist them to learn how to be happy in life.

Richard spent many happy days hiking in national parks, crawling over boulders, and peering at Indian pictographs. He toured the Channel Islands off Santa Barbara and stared in fascination at wasps building their homes in Anza-Borrego. One of his joys is photography, and he has photographed more than 1,200 belly dancing events, as well as dozens of Renaissance fairs all over the country.

Because writing is his passion, Richard remains incredibly creative and prolific; each day he writes between 5,000 and 10,000 words, diligently using language to bring life to the world so that others may learn and be entertained.

Richard is the CEO of The Writing King, which specializes in fulfilling any writing need. You can find out more at https://www.thewritingking.com/, and emails are welcome at rich@thewritingking.com

Books by Richard G Lowe Jr.

Business Professional Series

On the Professional Code of Ethics and Business Conduct in the Workplace – Professional Ethics: 100 Tips to Improve Your Professional Life - have you ever wondered what it takes to be successful in the professional world? This book gives you some tips that will improve your job and your career.

Help! My Boss is Whacko! - How to Deal with a Hostile Work Environment - sometimes the problem is the boss. There are all kinds of managers, some competent, some incompetent, and others just plain whacked. This book will help you understand and handle those different types of managers.

Help! I've Lost My Job: Tips on What to do When You're Unexpectedly Unemployed – suddenly having to leave your job can be a harsh and emotional time in your life. Learn some of the things that you need to consider and handle if this happens to you.

Help! My Job Sucks Insider Tips on Making Your Job More Satisfying and Improving Your Career – sometimes conditions conspire to make the regular trek to a job feel like a trip through Dante's Inferno. Sometimes, these are out of our control, such as a malicious manager or incompetent colleague. On the other hand, we can take control of our lives and workplace and improve our situation. Get this book to learn what you can do when your job sucks.

Books by Richard G Lowe Jr.

How to Manage a Consulting Project: Make money, get your project done on time, and get referred again and again – I found that being a consultant is a great way to earn a living. Managing a consulting project can be a challenge. This book contains some tips to help you so you can deliver a better product or service to your customers.

How to be a Good Manager and Supervisor, and How to Delegate – Lessons Learned from the Trenches: Insider Secrets for Managers and Supervisors – I've been a manager for over thirty years I learned many things about how to get the job done and deliver quality service. The information in this book will help you manage your projects to a high level of quality.

Focus on LinkedIn – Learn how to create a LinkedIn profile and to network effectively using the #1 business social media site.

Home Computer Security Series

Safe Computing is Like Safe Sex: You have to practice it to avoid infection – Security expert and Computer Executive, Richard Lowe, presents the simple steps you can take to protect your computer, photos and information from evil doers and viruses. Using easy-to-understand examples and simple explanations, Lowe explains why hackers want your system, what they do with your information, and what you can do to keep them at bay. Lowe answers the question: how to you keep yourself say in the wild west of the internet.

Books by Richard G Lowe Jr.

Disaster Preparation and Survival Series

Real World Survival Tips and Survival Guide: Preparing for and Surviving Disasters with Survival Skills – CERT (Civilian Emergency Response Team) trained and Disaster Recovery Specialist, Richard Lowe, lays out how to make you, your family, and your friends ready for any disaster, large or small. Based upon specialized training, interviews with experts and personal experience, Lowe answers the big question: what is the secret to improving the odds of survival even after a big disaster?

Creating a Bug Out Bag to Save Your Life: What you need to pack for emergency evacuations - When you are ordered to evacuate—or leave of your free will—you probably won't have a lot of time to gather your belongings and the things you'll need. You may have just a few minutes to get out of your home. The best preparation for evacuation is to create what is called a bug out bag. These are also known as go-bags, as in, "grab it and go!"

Professional Freelance Writer Series

How to Operate a Freelance Writing Business, and How to be a Ghostwriter – Proven Tips and Tricks Every Author Needs to Know about Freelance Writing: Insider Secrets from a Professional Ghostwriter – This book explains how to be a ghostwriter, and gives tips on everything from finding customers to creating a statement of work to delivering your final product.

How to Write a Blog That Sells and How to Make Money From Blogging: Insider Secrets from a Professional Blogger:

Books by Richard G Lowe Jr.

Proven Tips and Tricks Every Blogger Needs to Know to Make Money – There is an art to writing an article that prompts the reader to make a decision to do something. That's the narrow focus of this book. You will learn how to create an article that gets a reader interested, entices them, informs them, and causes them to make a decision when they reach the end.

Books by Richard G Lowe Jr.

Other Books by Richard Lowe Jr

How to Be Friends with Women: How to Surround Yourself with Beautiful Women without Being Sleazy – I am a photographer and frequently find myself surrounded by some of the most beautiful women in the world. This book explains how men can attract women and keep them as friends, which can often lead to real, fulfilling relationships.

How to Throw Parties like a Professional: Tips to Help You Succeed with Putting on a Party Event – Many of us have put on parties, and I know it can be a daunting and confusing experience. In this book, I share what I learned from hosting small house parties to shows and events.

Additional Resources

Is your career important to you? Find out how to move your career in any direction you desire, improve your long-term livelihood, and be prepared for any eventuality. Visit the page below to sign up to receive valuable tips via email, and to get a free eBook about how to optimize your LinkedIn profile.

http://list.thewritingking.com/

I've written and published many books on a variety of subjects. They are all listed on the following page.

https://www.thewritingking.com/books/

On that site, I also publish articles about business, writing, and other subjects. You can visit by clicking the following link:

https://www.thewritingking.com

To find out more about me or my photography, you can visit these sites:

Personal website: https://www.richardlowe.com
Photography: http://www.richardlowejr.com
LinkedIn Profile: https://www.linkedin.com/in/richardlowejr
Twitter: https://twitter.com/richardlowejr

If you have any comments about this book, feel free to email me at rich@thewritingking.com

Premium Writing Services

Do you have a story that needs to be told? Have you been trying to write a book for ages but never can seem to find the time to get it done? Do you want to brand your business, but don't know how to get started?

The Writing King has the answer. We can help you with any of your writing needs.

> **Ghostwriting**. We can write your book, which entails interviewing you to get your story, writing the book and then working with you to revise it until complete. To discuss your book, contact The Writing King today.
>
> **Website Copy**. Many businesses include the text on their sites as an afterthought, and that can result in lost sales and leads. Hire The Writing King to review your site and recommend changes to the text which will help communicate your message and improve your sales.
>
> **Blogging**. Build engagement with your customers by hiring us to write a weekly or semi-weekly article for your blog, LinkedIn or other social media. Contact The Writing King today to discuss your blogging needs.
>
> **LinkedIn**. LinkedIn is of the most important vehicles for finding new business, and a professionally written profile works to pulling in those leads. Write or update your profile today.
>
> **Technical Writing**. We have broad experience in the computer, warehousing and retail industries, and have

Premium Writing Services

written hundreds of technical documents. Contact The Writing King today to find out how we can help you with your technical writing project.

The Writing King has the skills and knowledge to help you with any of your writing needs. Call us today to discuss how we can help you.

www.ingramcontent.com/pod-product-compliance
Lightning Source LLC
Chambersburg PA
CBHW060045230426
43661CB00004B/656